Cherubims

Cherubims

Poems by

Edward Clarke

© 2022 Edward Clarke. All rights reserved.
This material may not be reproduced in any form, published,
reprinted, recorded, performed, broadcast,
rewritten or redistributed without
the explicit permission of Edward Clarke.
All such actions are strictly prohibited by law.

Cover design by Shay Culligan
Cover art by Jörg Bittner Unna - Own work, CC BY 3.0

ISBN: 978-1-63980-235-7

Kelsay Books
502 South 1040 East, A-119
American Fork, Utah 84003
Kelsaybooks.com

For Francesca, Ludovico, and Iacopo

Acknowledgments

Acknowledgements are due where poems in this collection have previously appeared:

Cassandra Voices: "The Firstborn," "Assembly"
E-Verse Radio: "The Tantrum"
The North American Anglican: "The Parable of the Vineyard"
The Spectator: "First Snow," "The Naked Limbs"
Spiritus: "Christmas"
The Voice inside Our Home (Oxford: SLG Press, 2022): "The Idiom of the Psalms," "Cherubs," "Cherubim," "My Vision of Two Cherubim," "Holy, Holy, Holy," "Tetramorph," "Christmas," "The Journey," "Plate 21"

I would like to thank those who read versions of these poems along the way, especially Mark S. Burrows, Anthony Caleshu, David and Sherille Clarke, Andy and Nassim Cooke, Julia Craig-McFeely, Ned Denny, Susan Gillingham, Emma and Paul Griffin, Ernest Hilbert, David Jasper, Francis Leneghan, Enrico and Dariel Magnabosco, Don S. Martin, Jamie McKendrick, Nathaniel Mellors, Enrico and Elena Racca, and Annette and Frank von Delft.

I am grateful to Karen Kelsay and the staff at Kelsay Books for their hand in the making of this book.

Contents

I

First Snow	17
The Toddler Is God	18
The Scroll Bar	19
The Parable of the Vineyard	20
Lament, or Lullaby	21
Goodrich Castle	23
No Common Measure	24
Taddei Tondo	25
Via della Domus Aurea	26
Hymn to Hermes	27
Against the End of Day	28
Compositional Sketch	29

II

The Firstborn	33
Osmosis	35
The Naked Limbs	36
No World without Us	37
The Brothers	38
Cherubims	40
Di sotto in sù	42
The Bunk Bed	43
Annette's Version	44
Delphica	46
The Tantrum	47
His Soft Cheetah	48
The Idiom of the Psalms	49

III

The Morning Routine	53
My Vision of Two Cherubim	54
The Leaven	56
My Fall and Recovery	58
Bettelgedicht	59
My Old *Concise*	60
Striguil	61
The Willow	62
Cherubs	63
The Purloined Pearl	64
School Assembly	65
Annunciation	66
Christmas	67
La Befana	69
The Flight into Egypt	70

IV

Eight Sonnets	75
Holy, Holy, Holy	83
On Matter	85
Tetramorph	86
Ex forti dulcedo	87
The Amethyst	88
A Small Torso	89
Waste Ground	90
The Picnic	91
Foxtails	92

V

The Ground of the Soul	95
The Apartment	96
Visitation	97
The Infinite Sum	99
The Great Threshold	100
No Picnic	101
No Mercy Seat	102
Sphinges	103
Initiation	106
Navicularius	107
Zoomorphism	108
Contentation	109
The Night	110
The Hunt for the Soul	111
The Net	112
Steel	113
The Marriage	114
Of the End of the World	115
Plate 21	116
Banqueting House	117

So he drove out the man; and he placed at the east of the garden of Eden Cherubims, and a flaming sword which turned every way, to keep the way of the tree of life.

Genesis 3:24

Briefly then, cherubin, cherubins *are the original English forms, as still in French. But, in the process of Biblical translation,* cherubin *has been supplanted by* cherub; *and* cherubins *has been 'improved' successively to* cherubims, cherubim; *while, concurrently,* cherub *has been popularly fitted with a new plural* cherubs.

"cherub," *Oxford English Dictionary*

I

First Snow

I have in mind a snapshot of our son
Upheld by you in a prospect of snow,
Taken when he was less than half of one
On a cold mountain seven years ago.
It was the first snow he was ever shown,
Was blinded by and touched, and his cheeks glow.
His puffer suit is white. His hat is green.
Clearly the sky's unmixed ultramarine.

And I recall he slept a long time after,
Upright in the car seat I'd pulled from the jeep
And stood up underneath the cabin's rafters,
So we could eat a long lunch during his sleep
And he'd not hear the clatter of our laughter
While we'd in Vin Santo our biscuits steep.
He left no footprints in the snow that day
But made yours somewhat deeper I would say.

The Toddler Is God

I mutter almost anything
Before your plush bedraggled stuff,
      And every morning think,
Tomorrow's fine, today's enough.
I count the precious syllables,
Before you rise, set something down.
The silent treasured animals
              Hear no sound.

Brought down you struggle in my arms
And take the shapes of elephant
      And fox, one moment calm,
The next most like a weather front
At dusk that splits sunset to shards:
Pink lightning plies where geese just flew,
Suddenly the potholes spew
           Old puddles upwards.

When you're not here I rearrange
Your mess, put toys and things away:
      Your vast upheavals changed
To cold, nostalgic, tidy days;
Someone speaks of you, my heart
Turns inside its cot and moans
And coughs a moment, sleeps to dawn,
           By fits and starts.

The Scroll Bar

My thumb on the scroll bar, I watch days run
Through holiday snaps, milestones, and the odd
Day out, the first full year of my first son.

From Christmas beach to Christmas beach, my God,
How they race, with flashes of scowls and twinkling looks,
On carousels and swings, and down paths trod

When I'd gone back for the monkey he forsook.
Before a plaster-cast Laocoön
I see his face; I see him smile at a book,

Then out a pumpkin suit, then Advent's gone:
I see these things, and sense our days are spun,
And so we're raised at last, like stones thrown down.

The Parable of the Vineyard

          It's said his last words were
Unto the uttermost part of the earth,
                  My place of birth,
                  And standing there,
      I gaze upon a cloud
And wish to high heaven that he'd come out.

          I look steadfastly on
His witnesses: clear windows fused with light
                  And heads long gone
                  By walls washed white,
And wish the flèche-consuming Holy Ghost,
                The flames of Pentecost,

          Would fuel my utterance too.
I lean on my dormer window to listen for
                Your foot on the floor,
                But there's no shoe-
            Less hymn this May Day morn,
Just ring road traffic taking the wings of dawn.

          What is this house that I've
Made up for you just by my living in it?
                Were you alive,
                  Would it be finished?
You went to a far country for a long time,
            But left us this stone, and lime.

Lament, or Lullaby

Too old to drive to Aldi,
He let us have his Ford,
Whose window seals grew mouldy
And whose analogue dashboard
Soon blared with different tunes
To the marches and muzak
We found one afternoon
In an armrest's tape rack:
This man who loved a jest
And even on his deathbed
Laughed to hear it confessed
We hadn't washed his car yet,
Whose slippers I'd filled with mud
When I was a shy child
And felt along my blood
A wildness when he smiled:
This man who can't be hushed,
Whose fan is in his hand
And whose throat's distended, flushed
With cries, like those the damned
Let out, to punctuate
Recurring cadences
In tunes that fluctuate
From that, which distances
Itself beyond the plains:
Wild curly passages
Like oriental strains,
Which might at last assuage us.
Sweet son who clasps the car seat's
Handle in elation,
What is it flits and fleets
Through Mary's generations
And babbles back to me

Celestial lullabies,
What is it that you see
Compels the genii
Along the world's byways
These dwindling August days.

Goodrich Castle

From the ruined top of a light grey sandstone keep
The footage rolls clockwise: a mother sees
She's filmed and waves with her child; you can hear sheep

In the luscious valley, birds in emerald trees.
The tower's late Norman, circled by pink rings
Of Gothic walls. There's hardly a May breeze.

Two days before, like sheaves an autumn flings
Off its land, we saw my mother's father laid
In a suit the shade of limestone knights and kings.

Time comes, then turns and waves, as if we're made
Of days and months and years only to be reaped.
Bright child, for a day in your courts what wouldn't I trade?

No Common Measure

If there's a proper dignity—
        Proportion to be observed—
In every act of life, they say,
        Then what's this thing that's severed

Me today from all my chores?
        This force that bounces naked
Towards the borders of my bed,
        Its interference sacred

As the rising of the Dog Star
        Above the Nile in August:
This child that throws itself or socks off
        The balcony, or almost.

The sun behind the sun pronounces
        Dampness and then bikini
Before tossing it to the compost
        And the flowers of zucchini

We really should have fried and eaten
        Only yesterday.
The Word behind the words and lines
        I've tried all day to say

Still has me hover here to catch
        Its possibilities
And hold to the page the child's play
        Of all philosophies.

Between the rising of the Dog Star
        That brings the river's treasure
And anyone's hypotheses
        There is no common measure.

Taddei Tondo

The day before the shortest day I snapped
A shot of you holding our lurching son
Like Mary in the Taddei Tondo, lapped

By the folds of the Mediterranean.
Four minutes later, he was in my arms,
And you composed a tableau of us alone

Against a sea the visitant clouds can't quite calm
In their exuberant greys with strokes of gold.
I must have been conceiving of a psalm,

One of the first I made, as waves are rolled
In turquoise to the shore, and at the bay's cap
The sky thrusts out a bird it strives to hold.

Via della Domus Aurea

In this cold room my memory would evoke
A picture of you by oleanders, pines
And cypresses, and one bellied holm oak

Whose back seems turned to the gold god that shines
Through upper arches of the broken O
Below. I see this shot's displayed online

As your icon, and I choose it, even though
I have a hundred others of you at home
Or in fields by our house where we like to go.

If those domestic scenes were put in this poem
And that poem in this book, it would be we awoke
In a golden house thrown open to all of Rome

And I'd divulged the master who applies
Paint to intonaco smoothed just for your eyes.

Hymn to Hermes

Your mother basks like a knoll to which labourers come
But the next shot's a blur of blue sheets scrunched
And then you're lifted out the incised womb

With legs drawn up as if you're caught mid-plunge;
I see you then wailed at your mum, before
You were weighed, then fed with milk for your first lunch.

I scroll through my snaps, and you're soon on the floor
And off, not long in the cradle before you longed
To make music, taste meat, and try the door.

Transplanted, watered with Apollo's songs,
You move as a thief through the mandorla of our home,
But feign sleep when the god comes to say he was wronged.

Against the End of Day

Inside the almond shell of sleep,
        On overlapping nights,
A baby's cry triangulates
        The valley's stream and heights.

Another commands capriciously
        And cannot be appeased:
We come and go upon blind feet
        Already ill at ease.

Our days are strewn as if they are
        A squirrel's heart-shaped husks.
A blackbird sings of brushes laid
        Beside the gesso dusks.

Against the end of day, we lean
        Our implements a while:
We're easily distracted by
        An old tale, or tiny smile.

Compositional Sketch

You sit, a pyramid amid toys strewn
On playmat and floorboards, hold one son up
As on a page of studies for a cartoon,

And let the smaller one wail in your lap.
Your head is tilted back, and light is glanced
Off it from a window, which angels tap,

Eager to frame your form with slender hands
And wings of garden birds. (One might suppose,
Could this shot be so re-composed, it chanced

The phone's scroll bar stopped at.) Your eyes are closed,
Your smile's serene, and in the fullness of June
You radiate the year from crown to toes.

II

The Firstborn

      I thought I would read the book beginning
          In the beginning was
          The Word, and the Word was . . .
But the pages opened at the book beginning
          The book of the generation . . .
      And I built my poem on that foundation.

      My intention was to write about
          A father and a son
          Hand in hand upon
A curving shore, and although now I doubt
          This happened word for word
      It can stand for what really occurred.

      Those early summer evenings spent
          With my dad on that outcrop
          Watching peregrines drop,
Or in the woods, off way-marked paths, intent
          To find the fabled stand
      Of Weymouth Pines, which we, at last, found.

      Our lingering at Mickla Bridge,
          Discoursing about Yeats,
          As the sun politely waits
To set behind the bluing fields' high ridge.
          My making my arm a cushion
      For my son's head to dream and push on.

      But while I thought on these things, behold,
          An angel of the Lord
          Appeared beside this word
And told me all he'd heard of that household
          Conceived of the Holy Ghost,
      And his words were the multitude of a host.

What have I written? And what have I
            Imagined and not written?
            And what remains unwritten
And unimagined in this poem? Before I
            Knew it, my thoughts were lost,
      Or found with child of the Holy Ghost.

Osmosis

       Spontaneously, I'm told,
       From out the heavy commotion
          Of my household
And your heavenly book, a substance rises
         Into a stranger solution
Contained in roots that I have put
       Into them, and so passes
          In its osmosis
   Into these leaves and fruit.

       This solvent nothingness,
       Which must process from root
          To fruitfulness,
Sits up to no breakfast and throws
       No bowl at his brother, who'd
Not throw it back in any case,
         And what is written knows
           That there it goes
   Like a poem on for days:

       Three hours, or less, of writing,
       And then a day, or three,
          Of the usual fighting,
And making up, and getting ready
       For school and nursery,
Or work; then coming home again
         With feet and clothing muddy
            And that blackened teddy,
   Lost, like a put-down pen.

The Naked Limbs

You told me that you'd read,
And were struck by
That night in bed,
A sermon on the naked limbs that lie
Inside your soul,
And as you told me so,
Our youngest son, whose loud voice cried, rushed
Usurpingly to climb
Inside our sheets and quilt, with soaked pyjamas
Stripped just in time,
And tears as suddenly stopped and hushed
As those of laments and psalms are.
He mumbles to your heart in bed:
You will lay him down when he is quieted.

A pair of labouring rhymes
Can hardly mould
This son who climbs
Inside our bed into the form of a soul,
And, stripped of thought,
Show it nakedly caught
In the arms of God. This son whom we have made
Is just somewhat like us,
Whereas the soul up there is what it climbs:
A nothingness
Matched by everything that God has laid
Aside of God to hold its limbs.
Such a son, made before we kissed,
Lies still in bed, a naked atheist.

No World without Us

What is this medium through which life drifts?
                What is the point of it?
                              And what if no sons
Or daughters come to slow the days and months
                It takes for years to flit
                              Like swallows and swifts?

We think we can imagine this world without us.
                That trees shall sprout and span
                              These rooms, which fill
With fallen glass and their own walls, until
                There's just our pots and pans
                          In the detritus.

But we'd be wrong to try and imagine thus:
                To think our chemicals
                              Shall be absorbed
As rivers run to depollute this orb
                To its hot core, and all
                              That's left of us

Are millions and millions of tyres
                And buried metal things;
                            Our plastics all
Disintegrated into particles,
                An ocean species brings
                          Itself to devour.

Let every soul recall, instead, what's born
                Inside us all to rend
                            This lovely veil
The world, to make, like a coat in some old tale,
                The words we'll wear in the end
                            When all things are torn.

The Brothers

I

        And when he'd finished the poem
        To his old wife and friend
        His face was the face of an angel
        As it had been illumined.

        I've heard in the mouths of children
        The source text's melody.
        A whole vanful of them
        Under a graffitied tree.

        I could flesh out the details
        And cover up the theme.
        The naturalistic details
        I dreamed inside a dream.

The dressing up in capes and masks.
        The fighting with bright swords.
The playing with the girls next door.
        The wrestling when they're bored.

        But my words, they are corrupted,
        Compared to their lost sound.
The voice I've heard of a brother's blood
        That cries out from the ground.

There were two brothers in the north
        And one speaks through the other,
As he had been away at school,
        Not wrestling with his brother.

II
        A long-lost brother took my heel
            And pulled me screaming back
        Into the pitcher from the well
            Upon our mother's back.
And in that barren space we struggled together
As changeable as seas in all kinds of weather.

        And I became the other's voice
            That cries out from the ground,
        Through which the roots of trees rejoice
            With their archaic sound
Of psaltery and harp: my language here,
A word of praise eternally in your ear.

        A starry elemental man
            Who steps out from your heart,
        Whose soul is in the groundless span
            Of your enlightening art,
I rush to greet you now and pull you out
Into the freshest suspension of pitch-black doubt.

Cherubims

I contemplate this room
And it looks a bloody mess, the carpet strewn
      With bits of stuff,
      Unvacuumed fluff,
And my dried-up mind that lies inside it,
A flash flood, which left its fulness on the walls
      As it departed, all
Our things sullied and redeposited.

      The beings that made this mess
In their most high and eternal dance of excess
      Of knowledge of God
      Might think it odd
I'm not so lifted up into the light
Of their kind of composite contemplation
      In superabundant elation
As I sit here making them so childlike.

      But then they do not think
As I pretend to do when these words drink
      Them in and are freed.
      They cannot read
Even the words set forth in holy scripture.
They are so filled with light their minds are blind
      To what is on my mind:
The landscape of its naturalistic picture.

      They are of the highest order
And can but, on the snowy ridge of that border,
      Participate
      And imitate,
As close to Christ as my two boys when they're
Tickled before bedtime and they behold
      As cherubims of old
The face of your deepest radiance everywhere.

        I look for the text of their hymns
So I might surpass these radiant cherubims,
                But find the scroll
                Is lost, the whole
Of it, they say, even a fabrication.
But then the floorboards creak above, I hear
            A waking yawn, and peer
At a song hurriedly transcribed in elation.

Di sotto in sù

My arms are held half-raised, my neck is craned,
        Beside this climbing frame,
Poised to catch the tumbling heads and bums
        Of these my poems, or sons.
I could be peering at an oculus
        Painted up above us:
A cherubimed space through which sweet pranksters watch
        Their court become a hodgepodge
For thousands now to taste of, ever chaste
        Above the lost estates.
But then the sun comes out and suddenly it seems
        An aureate nakedness gleams
All along the sky's entablature
        Beyond any azure ladder.
The frame is wobbling as the cherubim
        Together climb and climb
Around the anterooms of highest heaven
        To be uplifted even
Beyond the scenes that I see there of scripture,
        Or what my mind can picture.
One cries unto his brother and says through his tears
        What sounds inside my ears
As holy, holy, holy, is the Lord of hosts.
        I hold the trembling posts,
And a neighbour standing next to me says,
        Write a poem about this,
The radiant bums and heads above our heads
        And all our garden sheds.

The Bunk Bed

        My sons slept through the thunderstorms
            As I slept through a fear
        Of the Lord that booms around the Psalms,
Dreaming of an audience who'll hear
              Me recite tomorrow.
But such a dream only disintegrates
              In the rising sorrows
              Of saline time.
        Let him that fears the Lord praise him
        And he shall inhabit such praise
With all the world's creatures for forty days.

        One day I'll wake and surely say,
            The Lord is in this place
And I knew it not, on my way
To anywhere but wrought heaven's high gates.
              And on that spot
I'll put the stones I'd taken for my pillows
              On the bed's plot
              And set them up
        For a pillar I'll pour oil on top.
        I'll take my harp down from its willow
And call to this dry place all thy waves and billows.

        Although we sleep like logs, they said,
            We've ears that can hear lightning.
        My two small sons, on their bunk bed,
Are forever ascending and descending
              The dream of my poems,
Before they wake to alter suppositions
              Made inside them,
              And these logs will do,
        I thought, as a simile to hew,
        To make some nests, or rooms, for my visions,
Which I shall coat with pitch in sedulous fashion.

Annette's Version

Über alle Erkenntnis soll man kommen
Was Cherubin *erkennt, das mag mir nicht genügen.*
Ich will noch über ihn, wo nichts erkannt wird, fliegen.
  —Angelus Silesius, *Cherubinischer Wandersmann,* 1:284

What the cherub knows, she began,
Or understands, that is not enough for me,
Or sufficient, not sufficient, for me. And then, bang,
    A curly cherub of mine
    Tumbles from the trampoline
    With singular intensity
To make his harshly supplicating hymn
    For me to tickle him.

I take my neighbour's version down
Before I take my son up in my arms:
I am seeking to exceed him, she says, and frowns,
    To fly over his knowledge
    (I'm sorry this isn't very polished)
    Into the unknown space. Alarmed
By her daughter's screams, I note, *Beyond gnosis*
    One has to strive, as she closes

The book. How could that epigram
Be made to stay in just my poem's first stanza,
I thought, as I take back my book, and, bam,
    My son jumps to a chair
    Whose arm he climbs as into the air.
    Like a putto on a ledge, he stands there:
A boisterous form who straightens out my soul,
    As it leaves such words as *soul.*

The intelligence that purifies
Grotesque angelic forms in Ezekiel,
As it is emptied out and divinized

In the writing of its book,
Takes up the sword of our last look
At Eden, and, to make it real,
Turns it to what's to come, is, and has been,
And never can be seen.

Delphica

    Half-way through or the end of walks
        Or even for a bit
    At the beginning to get us moving,
        I'd lift a son to sit
Upon my shoulders, where he'd watch the street
        Or field or hills at my feet.

    At first it was the force I felt
        Of our radiant blond son
    And then the growing limbs and bum
        Of the darker curly one,
Who is so strongly my own image, he
        Is a kind of mini-me;

    Like the dark genius whispering
        Over the shoulder of Joel,
    One end of Michelangelo's ceiling,
        And looking at his scroll:
The shadowiest of his cherubim,
        A full-haired mini-him.

    Were I to prophesy and write
        The cherub's text, I'd seem
    As drunk as Noah on his farm
        With visions or dreams to dream:
I would be wild as *Delphica,* wide-eyed
        In a furor a god could ride.

The Tantrum

The sound upon my shoulders,
Upon the mountain roads,
Beside the many channels of waters,
Seemed like a prayer of God's
That pulled my hair and cried into my ears
In its distress and fears.

And from its secret place
Darkness purified
The cherub it rode to scatter and chase
That against which it cried:
With lightning disbelief was discomfited,
My head struck and perfected.

Hailstones and coals of fire,
I thought, I'll have to put
This child down and his unquenchable ire,
And let him walk our route,
Or stand and scream his tantrum off to the earth
That shook because of his wrath.

But, no, I kept him there,
And let my head be struck,
Again, and again, with his wild prayer,
And thought, with any luck
He'll pull through this crying, and I'll be brought
Above the refuge of thought.

His Soft Cheetah

   Despite a rising tropological fear
Playfully I cast myself as Abraham that morning
       My son stood staring and yawning
As we packed rucksacks with chocolate and mountain gear
         And his soft cheetah,
And now that I recall our journey to that place
    Of which I'd told him high above the lakes
      I strain to keep to this metre.

   My fear's realized as I become less kind
To this poem, which seems so like a radiant son
       Whom I have bound upon
The darkness of unknowing: all that the fixed mind
        Conceives, which I'd
Put in it, stares at me in its silence and prays
   For a ram in a bush, or a rhyme that stays
      My hand; the Lord will provide.

The Idiom of the Psalms

        Last night our eldest son
        Was anxious to relate
    An anecdote our youngest one
Would take and twist and quite exaggerate,
Repeating this detail, changing that phrase,
      To regale those listening for a lesson
        With parallel cola of praise
            Of divine effervescence.

        The eldest set a scene
        Of heavy rain, when, lo,
    The youngest jumped in, said he'd seen
Big thunderstorms, and conjured up clouds, low
On hills that fizzed and shook, and darkness round
      The earth that billowed in the noise;
        The floods have lifted up their sound:
            The floods lift up their voice.

        Can it be that they're charmed
        And magically upraised
    To speak the idiom of the Psalms?
They seem to live, like trees, at the height of praise,
These boys, and when that tale was done, they bashed
      Cymbals and synthesizer to make
        Tunes louder than all waves that crash
            For their grandparents' sake.

III

The Morning Routine

You rage because your socks are not quite right,
        Or when your pants are hitched tight,
    And when it's clearly warm outside,
            You'll not believe
                Today's short sleeves,
    Let alone shorts. Your brother hides
          Behind the door, stands naked,
His soul's functions unexpressed, his nakedness sacred.

You come down counting risers on our stair,
        Find twelve have been fixed there,
    And suddenly our house, like this verse,
           Becomes a walk-in
           And fully working
    Model of the universe,
        Seen in conformity
With Christ's conception of our family.

After breakfast, solving maths exercises,
        Like mysteries of Isis
    Or those of Mary, you number spots
           On a cartoon snake,
              Whose sinews make
      Their way coaxingly across
          The page, then cast small bricks
To a pile you estimate is two times six.

And as for the other his feet had almost slipped
        As he charged and almost tripped,
    Half-dressed on the stair, still refusing
           To eat breakfast.
           As a die's cast
    To find a square not of your choosing,
        So this line tumbles south
To its six and the player goes past rung and snake's mouth.

My Vision of Two Cherubim

I
         If, intent upon
             The balancing
        Of your bike through pedalling
        Yourself on, you are one
        Of the cherubim, and you turn
Your lion's face to me, those eyes that burn,
        When I let go of the saddle
        And you waver and topple
            Over those wheels
On which you've sat and waited and yet still move—
If you are, then, one of the cherubim,
        Whose weight the tarmac feels
            Like a brush with love,
        Or common measure hymn
The vast scene played and pedalled around you
        Is but a prelude to—
If you are one of these cherubim,
        Look at the girl next door,
            Who's just returned
From being away a month or more,
            And in one hour learned
        What you that month have burned to do,
And in five minutes you will do it too.

II
                If, intent upon
                        Emulating
        Your elder brother through taking
        The same bike three years on
        And sitting on it, you are
The other cherub, and rage at a parked car,
        Or when the path is rough,
        Not when I let go so much—
            If you are that cherub,
Look upon the road ahead, right there,
And marvel. For in your wheels your spirit moves,
        That precious moment whereof
            You're not aware,
        But my bent back loves,
When you are cycling alone and the birds clap,
        And I can straighten up.
    With circling feet like sparkling hooves,
        You speed, not after your brother,
            But as one
    That springs at once from out the other,
        Here and gone.
    And withersoever the brothers went,
Thither the wheels go, under the firmament.

The Leaven

It's all too easy to say, we are tired,
        And do not mean all that we say,
            But some realities
    Can only be put in this way,
              When we are wired
            And cross and mild
As contradicting genealogies
        Woken to hold their newborn child.

Before the dawn, or ever the earth was,
        I see you are a thought of earth,
            Then earth itself, and daily his
    Delight, after your second birth,
              Which made you wise
            And an helpmeet.
Later I hear you cry, at the doors of our house,
        Come and wash your hands and eat.

I feel I met you first in a time of drouth:
        A damsel with a pitcher on
            Her back, from which I drank,
    When I'd gone near and rolled the stone
              From the well's mouth.
              One dawn, inside
A tent we'd struggled to pitch as the sun sank,
        I slept with you awake by my side.

Pacing upon the heights of my roof top,
        I see a woman washing herself,
            And know that I'll contrive
    To have her all to myself,
              And so raise up
              The name of the dead
Inside our house, for as long as we're alive,
        And climb in sickness and health to bed.

As with sourdough, I am left out and proved
        With those hard questions you have asked
              In your heart, and find my words
      Are lifted up by them at last,
                As by what moved
              At first on the deep:
I'd serve them to you, like many things you've heard,
      But cannot touch that good part you keep.

My Fall and Recovery

I swerved, when I beheld a man stand,
        And looked, and saw, a drawn sword
                In his raised hand,
        As captain of the host of the Lord,
Who had me fall on my face to the ground,
Over two bars, in one sudden bound.

As one or two passed by, I picked my watch,
        My bike, and my prone self, up from
                The ground, on which
        My blood dropped, thinking, I'll go home.
With a newborn Word asleep in her sling,
A mother asks if I need anything.

And when my nose was staunched, I latched my chain
        Back on its teeth, and cycled on,
                Discovering pain,
        Not knowing the skin of my face shone,
Until I came back home and saw the fear
Of my youngest son who wouldn't come at all near.

It was a fall to break the fallow ground
        From whence I was taken once, whose
                Impact was found
        Impressed upon my lip and nose
As water breaks the images, we see
Across it, of bank and upside-down tree.

Bettelgedicht

      Would anyone deny these little ones a treat?
What if they knock where there's a light but no grotesque and ask?
      They're dressed as little witches, skeletons, and ghosts,
And set out cheerfully enough, with faces painted or masked,
                         On their sweet task.

      A squash is gouged, given eyes, nose and teeth, and lit,
And children flock to the front door, but if no face is found
      And brightly displayed, it's useless for you to wait
For all these little ones to make, with little fists that pound,
                         Your door sound.

      My eldest son comes in when our front door is opened.
He shrinks himself before my legs, his nose against my knees,
      And when he's asked, what is the matter, he looks about,
Takes off his mask, and pleads to, clearly sad and ill at ease,
                         Stay here please.

      For every house that's lit its tempting Jack O'Lantern
Another few express blankly their incredulity.
      As my son stares in such an unfathomable manner,
So most my poems chuck eggs and flour then come to glare at me
                         Accusingly.

My Old *Concise*

I sit and make some ancient words
>Into a long-lined poem
As the winds bang and the rain rains
>Against a just-sold home,
And want to ask, out of whose womb came this weather?
>And has the rain a father?

At long last a stanza's finished:
>I look up from my page,
And see my son's face and my own
>At just about his age,
And photographs of cousins in uniform,
>On the sill before the storm.

My son comes down to the packed room
>And fingers a box of deeds,
Then takes a book, which opens at
>The letter *F,* and reads,
Haltingly, *Front of head from forehead to chin,*
>My father listening.

Striguil

      Imagining a vast castle ablaze
With cheer on its cliffs, musicians in its keep,
      I turn my face to the wall and weep:
      As in the dank middle court
            Of words of praise,
Whose loss, and their patron, I can only lament,
      A prophet is stopped short,
And turns again to face the entertainment.

      If he could cry the shadow back
Ten degrees in its dial, he'd reawaken
      Those courtly pleasures we've forsaken
      And let sleep for too long, and rescue
           The heart that's racked
In its dungeon, for it is bad to forget
      What men had once sworn to:
There is no green thing, the waters are desolate.

      For the sickness I am cured of,
I need no lump of figs, no medicine,
      But what I see, I pull and spin,
      And grasp again at both ends,
           And fling above:
Like a well-intended song of abuse, or praise,
      A scholarly poet sends
To a king, you'll play it too, one of these days.

      This much I can boast of: that I thought
I'd trouble myself to call that glory back
      From exile, whose city we've sacked,
      And sacked, time out of mind; that in
           This small house I bought
To rear my future boys, I'd tried to make
      A finer house, as thin
As days that on the deep blissfully break.

The Willow

      My little children make my days
      As thin as those of late October,
                And when they're over,
Those of November: playfully they chase
My life across a river and its border
                To a strange place,
Where women have a glamour, men are shorter.

      I stood with some around a font,
      The finest of whom were dressed up
                As at a nightclub
In just the kind of colours and textures I want
To make a song, or sonnet, like those of old;
                Mostly blonde,
Like primitive Marys, they looked proud and bold.

      My laden thoughts baulked when I heard,
      The text was, *Blessed are the poor.*
                Aloft at the door
Of a needle's eye, they're licked to the shape of a bird
And light on a suddenly steadfast tree.
                O, my word,
What roots are these? And through whose leaves do I see?

      My heart beats still inside its rings
      As a dove coos sweet nothings at
                The place where it's sat:
My green and silver canopy, which flings
On the rivers of water perpetual slivers of hair.
                Come see, it sings,
The opened treasures that're reflected there.

Cherubs

The cherubs sit along the bench,
    And swing their legs and sing,
The Lord's my shepherd, I'll not want,
    Their voices quavering,
As their eyes are led the quiet waters by
    An exact hand on high.

Sometimes it's dark, sometimes the sun
    Streams in from a high space,
As week by week these lively creatures
    Wind their crooked ways
Around the paths of righteousness, with a kind
    Of grace, or single mind.

Yea, though it rains or shines, they pay
    No mind, but watch that hand
That drives them to the sweetest tune
    Once heard in a far land:
They have a loving tendency to learn,
    Even though they bleat and squirm.

Copiously they pour their song
    On those who stand around,
Those notes they'll know forevermore,
    They lift as liquid sound,
And when the sweets are brought at last, they rush
    And choose in the church's hush.

The Purloined Pearl

It was a lollipop,
And not a pearl of great price,
We discovered you took from the small shop,
Around which you'd followed your mother,
Supplicating like a work of praise,
Or desperate, then furtive, lover.

But we were shocked enough,
As charmed, by this theft, the insolence
Of your greed and sweet tooth. You huffed and puffed
At our soft reprimand—
That finger like no flaming sword—but sensed,
No doubt, you're now beyond command.

Only the living can praise.
Tell that to the cherubim who keep
The way of the place of our origin. My days
Are usefully dark and short
In that they turn to me their face of the deep
To fetch down there what can't be bought.

School Assembly

One morning during the first week of Advent,
                        When I was possessed,
After a birthday's dark exhilarations,
        By a terrible kind of nervousness,
We saw, on stage, the judgement of our son,
Before his class, the Egyptian pantheon.

I was chosen, he said, to be mummified today:
                        My life was cut short
While I was out in my papyrus boat
        Hunting hippos (a dangerous sport).
Then they took the brains out of this son of ours,
And placed his viscera, like pasta, in cardboard jars.

As in the womb of Advent, I'd put myself
                        In that small space
In which they shut him, cured and bandaged up,
        And pray to God I feel the grace
Of Christmas, afloat inside its heavily
Expectant bustle, remote as a vessel at sea.

And what strange afterlife shall I find there,
                        On stage, when they lead
Me out, to weigh my heart against its feather?
        Wrapped in swaddling clothes and laid
In this book's manger, roughly I perceive
Angels, livestock, and men, the gifts you'll leave.

Annunciation

Although he writhed so fiercely on the couch
And made such an extravagant complaint,
The lines he had to learn stuck at one touch
Like pebbles dashed on lime or strokes of paint,
And no one seemed to doubt our son could play
The part of angel Gabriel on the day.

He missed rehearsals but showed no signs of alarm
When he was called to speak and everyone
Had eyes on him, and when he raised his arms
With imitation wings and surplice on,
Behold, the angel of our Lord appeared,
And he assuaged Mary and Joseph's fears.

The performance of those things Mary was told
Is itself an angel to behold in the form
Of slightly nervous five- to eight-year-olds:
He holds his hands like shepherds keeping warm
At an imaginary fire, and each prayer
Book's half put down as he is conceived there.

This poem came to angel Gabriel's mum
When he was cast, before she'd seen the play,
But the performance prompted me to hum
These words and finish it by Christmas day,
Hoping they stick to their lines as an eight-year-old
Whose face was the face of an angel to behold.

Christmas

I
I'd take the sheer expense of it,
The wailing kids in shopping malls,
That sausage roll that you just bit,
Those office girls against the walls,
And all their glasses of prosecco;
I'd take all this, and every gift
That gathers dust, unloved as Echo
By the coming year that cannot lift
Its gaze up from itself, I'd take
Them all, and your anxiety
Preparing lunch, the fights that break
Out eating it, the bad tv,
And pounds of fat you gain in front
Of it, in a state of indigestion
And then a somewhat somnolent
State of boredom; each cracker's question
And plastic toy and paper hat
That crowns old age's dozing off
Into its neck: I'd take all that,
And all such other Christmas stuff
We celebrate today, and bind
It fast, and flee to the heath of a place
As wild as I am, and hope what finds
Us there puts on its kindest face.
But what naked tree's this that grows
In this fresh space? Whose fingers are these
To touch the nose of lowing cows
That shall come in from winds that freeze?
As at the end of history
I hear the theme of a shepherd's song
As great as any mystery
To which all must come before long.

II
Since the angels went away to heaven,
                And cannot come again,
        The glory they seemed to take with them
                    Must still remain
In the shepherds' songs, who broke their watch in the night,
              For a thousand years in thy sight.

Long may it be found in the old philosopher's
                Question: *And how do we*
        Possess the divinity? who avers
                    We came to be
Constituted by a union
                Of the many and the one.

You said, *Let there be light,* and we came
                Thievishly after,
        And found our face to be the same
                    As yours, our laughter
As divine, at seeing it caught in a thousand mirrors,
              Or hatched with all our errors.

But Mary kept all these things, and pondered them
                In her heart, as the lit-
        Up eyes of my sons give now and then
                A glint of it:
The true light that shines in these, my long deferred,
              Uncomprehending words.

La Befana

You shined a star onto my hand,
Projected by the bedside lamp
You held in yours. Later that day, as I limped
Behind you on the street,
You turned and showed to me a small, red sweet,
You had purloined,
Which was the shape of a star,
While we were on our way to eat
At Stella Marina, where you played, outside the bar,
In a t-shirt's bold star.

I'd put the man who followed the star,
That moves still on the flickering face
Of that last stanza, into the close space
Of this one, so he can be
Refined to an elemental trinity
Of gifts from afar:
Those strangely precious crumbs
That are presented spontaneously
Out of the dark when the bald head at last succumbs
To the heart's fingers and thumbs.

But, oh, what coda is this that sweeps down on its broom
To leave its coal in a far corner of the room.

The Flight into Egypt

       Our journeys back from Italy
                  Always just after
     The big feast of Epiphany
                 Always seemed like
   A detail from a Flight
Into Egypt by a High Renaissance master.

     Until this year we would have had
               A wriggler on knee
   And shoulder; now they both watch an iPad,
              Suck lollipops,
          In case their ears pop:
My sons, at rest after two weeks with their *nonni*.

     A card the other set of grand-
              Parents sent me,
   Some years ago, which must still stand,
              Or lies, I think,
         Under mantelpiece junk,
Provides me with the image my heart can see:

     Of Mary and Child asleep on an ass
              Another son
   Of Joseph's angelically leads, her dress as
             Sumptuously painted
      As a king that's anointed,
With Joseph behind to goad his family on.

     In light of the poem I last wrote,
              Whose coda swept
   To me its coal, my father's hope,
              That my words may glow
        Like burning coal, seems somehow
Itself aglow, inscribed in that card I kept.

That card was a birthday card for me,
Born in Advent.
(My father on Epiphany.)
I have felt distressed,
But also strangely blessed,
As I goad this poem on to what's heaven sent.

IV

Eight Sonnets

I
While most of us might feel an impetus
To work Monday mornings, all children play,
And they will remonstrate and make a fuss
If asked to brush their teeth and start the day.
When mine come home from school they have a snack
Then rush to play again and only stop
If there's a fight or friends are ushered back:
They'd sooner play piano than tidy up.
The Persian rug's a plain of Lego shacks
And upturned cars and scattered pens and shoes;
By wheels of carriages and broken tracks
Stiff dragons lie like scrolls of lines and cues:
My sons come down and animate their wings;
In its fat suit or motley, the play sings.

II
My students shine as they have always shone
As by a sylvan pool and silver bather.
When I began, I could have married one,
But now I'm old enough to be her father.
Meanwhile my children grow so fast at home
They come to manifest the faithful years
That chase and hunt me down to the red loam
And throng around me in the pines and firs.
I stand and stare at frosted moonlit glass
At the same time tonight as yesternight
And there is fear in my heart that days pass
Continually with the night and take flight.
I know I am the sum of all my days
But words fail me as the air resounds with their bays.

III
My eldest son looked at our calendar
And pointed out the equinox had come
And gone the day before, when we were—doh—
Oblivious of it, and we were—um—
What were we doing when that moment passed?
It was half four, so we were stood outside
Our church, my eldest son came out his class,
My parents left, and we went for a joyride.
And where did we end up on that car trip?
We found a nursery where we bought mint
And native bluebells, snowdrops and cowslips,
While on their glide paths planes began to glint.
As we drove back past the airport, boughs blazed
Like candles lit to teach us and amaze.

IV
I vowed I'd sleep a reasonable night
Of sleep, but the rain came, and here I am
With a thousand thoughts I cannot quite put right,
Awake again at just past two a.m.
I pray our monolithic roof won't leak
And that it's just the scaffolding that drips,
And wonder if I teach the Chinese this week
And how I'll praise you without tongue and lips.
Can love string sounds together in the grave?
Does deconstruction end in truthfulness?
Whose tale is heard when earth's a drowning wave?
Whose faith survives this land's forgetfulness?
For countless nights I sealed the Psalms in my heart
And heard, or thought I heard, a cry in the dark.

V

Lichen is luminous to catch our eyes
And make them sing of it, while snowdrops come
In hope we'll praise them to the unsoiled skies
And pray the illuminated lines they hum.
Trees bend in penetrating air to hear
Tall tales of this year's leaves, while hedges smile
First smiles in hope a face comes cooing near
To theirs and stays to sing a rhyme awhile.
A robin alights on my fence, so I note him,
And the blackbird I heard before sunrise.
Since David died and Orpheus was torn limb
From limb, I say they sing, *who sees with our eyes,*
Who hears the primal psalm of all creation
It is your task to usher to completion.

VI

This month's a book you leaf through, pausing now
And then to scan those pieces you'd forgotten:
It seems so long ago, you wonder how
Those twigs and buds and flowers were ever written.
But what's this book, in which this poem is pressed,
Compared to the thorn's edible outburst
And the blackbird in whose song the dawn is dressed
And these bright flowers who put their hands up first?
The fox is in his den and crows hop by,
Then suddenly fly, with twigs clutched in their beaks,
But where shall this book find a place to lie?
Whose lap and hands are those its parched head seeks?
Each part of March performs its publication:
Each play forms part of a complete edition.

VII

She took our kids Good Friday afternoon
To ride a jet with them to Italy.
I stayed to teach Kyd's *Spanish Tragedy*
And Marlowe's *Doctor Faustus:* the first soon
Reread that day, the other watched with a moon
Moving above my study nakedly
Like a fine lady in a mystery
Or a dish run away with a rhyme's spoon.
That mad old Orphic father sees the face
Of his lost son in an incredulous
Man looking on; this scholar must have sensed
His years have been dramatically condensed.
My God, my God, have you forsaken us?
I ask myself as I prepare these plays.

VIII

They've wailed in their time through whole hymns and psalms
And ruined climaxes of homilies
With cries no picture book or biscuit calms
And would not offer any sign of peace.
But now with shy smiles they come processing
And sit together, standing up to chant
The *Kyrie* they have been practising,
Or sing, *The Lord's my shepherd, I'll not want.*
These children grow like thorns whose leaves I see
Before the rest: those sprouting in the apse
Shall make the choir a green and prosperous home.
These frisking kids flourish like the fig tree
Whose roots push up my poor patio slabs:
If they're contained, it's said, more fruit shall come.

Holy, Holy, Holy

I
When I come down to murmur out and test
My words against what rhymes must once have meant
      My intention is to match the hymns
          Sung by the seraphims
Whose glorious and encircling enlightenment
      Is thereby made manifest.

      I struggle to the ruined summit
      Of autobiographical verse
           And turn and hear the voice
                Of speech, like noise
      Of waters for a line to disperse,
          If I could only hum it.

          Blessed be the glory
          Of the Lord from this place
              Who thunders out
                  Like doubt
        Itself, or sun in your face,
          No absurd story,

              But holy, holy
              Holy, is
                  The Lord
              Of hosts. Yes,
                If only

                I could
                Match that,
                I would.

II
But when I come to read what I've produced
My lines appear to me like children's songs
       In a language I half-understand:
              The chorus swells, the band
Bursts out its horns, and my sons sing along
       To lyrics about tropical juice

       Or chocolate ice-cream and sweets.
       The car moved at the voice of their cry
          And now, as I recall
              Their singing, all
The house is filled with smoke and I
       Can feel the searing heat

          Of a live coal that's placed
          Upon my unclean lips.
             Woe is me!
              I see
      I shall cry, my fingertips
          Held to my face.

          I am undone.
          But here I am.
             Send me,
       A sweet-toothed man
             Whose tongue

            And lips
            Would sing,
            Or lisp.

On Matter

What is this shapelessness the mind conceives
Without the eye, which cannot meet the ear,
And has no savour or flavour when men eat,
Or body they might touch like yours or Eve's:
This basic stuff of all things on earth
Through which ideas are pulled to have their birth.

It seems to be like time itself in its
Elusiveness, a tarnished mirror of
Eternity, where all things must go off
Eventually, or be smashed to bits,
When the mirror's cracked at last, and you see each son
Leave home, each parent going, going, gone.

Sometimes this shapelessness appears to me
Like you yourself, a thing so difficult
To comprehend, but receptive to a fault
And in a beguiling way, quite easily
Ignited and fluid, but never quite fire or water,
Nor earth, nor air, as you stand and breathe as Eve's daughter.

What is it that's conceived in the soil of
These words that seems so full of promising love?

Tetramorph

What is this story I have read
                Over and over,
Whose events are, it's been said,
A manifest absurdity:
This tale that leaves us like a lover
To heartfelt incredulity,
And takes the head of the cherubims,
The better to speak with the voice of their hymns.

I've been too proud to pierce its sense,
                To listen for
Its manifold significance:
The truth inside that angel's book
Of the generations of Christ; that roar
Of one that cried with a wild look;
Or moved as an ox towards the trough;
That eagle, whose Word is enough.

He said, it is expedient
                I go away,
And since I know now that event
Is captured in the receptive cloud
Of its account, I'll try to say
Again, what I have been too proud
To see, or say, as I feel the pull
Of what is unpredictable:

That they are such as would grow up
                In little ones,
These holy scriptures, like a bear cub
A mother licks to shape, or these
Clods that mature to difficult sons,
Wholly enveloped in mysteries,
Who move to a point, that movement forms,
Without which they cannot be born.

Ex forti dulcedo

Now that I have begun to feel and choose
And pull the mouth of this poem's words, I don't doubt,
But I'll have need of her: my critical muse,
                Who can bring out
Of these, my opaque thoughts and stubborn lines,
A kind of sweetness like the queen bee's hoard
        Samson later found in the lion
Whose carcass he'd rent in the spirit of the Lord.

Sweet is the voice of all such criticism
That sounds like a dove in the clefts of the rock
And spills like light from a long-upheld prism:
                  That loved one's knock
Upon a stanza's door, without her key,
Expecting me to come and let her in there,
        Who sits herself down to take some tea,
Or puts a shoeless foot in the place of its stair.

I have a mind that would conceive of her
In such exuberance of thought it seems
To break the form I have established here.
                But as my dreams
Are thereby realized her very presence
Helps me recover, touch by touch, the sight
        Of natural things in my art: that essence
In which they're tucked, but they'd put off in the night.

The Amethyst

Our house is filled with your treasure,
All manner of precious stones
And pebbles almost beyond measure:
Quartz crystals, Fool's Gold and old thigh bones
You are convinced have hardened
Into the dinosaurs of our back garden.

Some of this stuff is all
That remains of the golden phase
Of my childhood, apart from a small
And tarnished cup, I'll polish one of these days,
And a bronze or dusky orange
Cat's eye I'd found loose on a road on Blorenge;

And one of the ammonites
Is one of my father's, I know,
But what were once ours, are now by rights
Yours, I would say, so keen are you to show
Your hoard and identify it
Even down to each piece of coal, or conglomerate.

My old collection provides
Foundation stones for this,
But still you came to me and cried
And implored I buy you an amethyst
Online for you to describe
In detail to distant friends once it's arrived.

Our house is filled too with tools
For shaping clay, paint brushes,
And scissors and glue: what takes my Fool's
Gold and Quartz; what artificer is it rushes
To consecrate this stuff,
Which hardly seems today, or tomorrow, enough.

A Small Torso

Here is a theme that wants to be expressed
        As a small torso above my head
Luxuriates and almost calls to be dressed,
Then yawns and rolls again upon its bed.
        Its warm feet jump upon the floor
Then rush severely along the corridor.

Who's this who waits above this room for me
        To notice him; to love and feed him,
Teach him to go; who's this, immediately
Climbed upon me as out of Egypt I'd lead him
        And take the yoke of that strange land
Off his jaw and lay his breakfast things to hand.

More sparingly shall you push your tiny cars
        On the floor, brumming them along;
And that bedraggled panda, cuddled hard
For years, shall lie at the foot of your bed among
        The other teddies. Less and less
Shall we hear it said, *Iacopo did this!*

This room is strewn with so many possibilities,
They lie like firewood to stack back to lit trees.

Waste Ground

Taken captive where I already am
I was lying by a brook of that waste ground,
      Just out of hearing of this spring's lambs
In sight of pylons beyond the empty playgrounds,
         When my sons brandished at me
     A vast invisible harp they'd found
Upon a branch of a willow's canopy.

You'd say I am imagining this harp,
That I'm making things up, but really there's
     No truer way to talk, and hark
About you now, you'll hear no finer airs
        To put words to than those
     Played on it when all your cares
Are tingling cunningly on fingers and toes.

The very words I bring forth now, if you'll
Believe in them, and the promises they make
     To you, are consubstantial
With those keen strings, whose notes are being raked
        In these edgelands of my soul,
     And as I lift and gently take
Them down they weigh like my sons off the bole.

As the appearance of a flash of lightning
Along the Devil's Backbone so my sons
     Are back on their bikes, frightening
And fierily enlivening at once
        All aloof passers-by:
     As breathless as a man that runs
Through willows and thorns, I call to them on high.

The Picnic

Behind a Kilner jar of wild red rice
      Upon our gaud- and card-strewn dresser
She tilts her face: the Virgin of the Rocks
      Whose hand is raised to calm or bless her
          Lolling son who sits
As prototype of ours on all our picnics.

If she'd look up, she'd spy the angels placed
      Behind the gazer's back, but like
Nature herself she reads the wishful face
      Of her child instead, to set him right
          And draw him back to herself:
Her concerns are his, his appetite itself.

And through dark rocks, or thrones and cherubims,
Our boys scramble into your unfolding limbs.

Foxtails

You bought a large lever arch file
To store the loose leaves of our son's
Maths homework, and for weeks now, I'll
Look up and see the foxes on
Its spine looking across the room at me
      Where I write imploringly.

They have the most beseeching faces
But seem rightly suspicious too
Of my implement, which starts and chases
Them to their hole, to put into
Their dumb mouth and most articulate maw
      A moral they'll abhor.

I reach for their *Aesopica*
While garnering material
To illustrate this poem, when, ah!
Three hundred foxes from their hole
Burn up with firebrand tails those shocks and sheaves
      I've bound under seared leaves.

I'll follow them whithersoever they head.
But the Son of man hath not where to lay his head.

V

The Ground of the Soul

      Just as I'm finishing my lunch
Almost every day just recently
      You call me to accompany you
Up to the back bathroom, where you'll sit hunched
      And with great energy
Push the same questions out, and some new ones too.

      What are made of, baths? "Cemarics"?
And wood? What is wood made of? Is it trees?
      And trees? What are trees made of? Wood?
I think of fibrous matter, tap ceramic
      Tops and surfaces
And wonder, can the bath be hardened mud?

      And then you make a cunning smile
And ask about humans and animals,
      And, three days later, books and words:
What are they all made of? You wonder while
      Initial principals
Draw answers up like angels or visiting birds.

      I sit and universalize
But you don't want to get back to the word go;
      Your questions are not quite the same
As your brother's whirring of incessant whys
      Around me years ago:
I sense you're playing a different kind of game.

      You have uncannily my hair
And face and so many things to say to me
      To which I cannot add the word God.
But I can see how we might get up there
      In words potentially
That rise as things I thought I understood.

The Apartment

My words are through the door and they're as errant
      And as playful and insolent
As my visiting offspring who seem intent
      On taking and wrecking their grandparents'
Stately apartment: sacks and chests of toys
Are upended by them, couches bounced on,
      And after the spectacular noise
            Of his meltdown,
The youngest puts a cloak on, points a gun,
      For sweets and biscuits, he'll never share.

My children charge from that stanza to this
      And back again repeatedly
And rush with shape-shifting intensity
      From this stanza to *nonna bis*.
But they shall need to hear a calming word
From me or her, if they're to make it higher
      Into this poem, to see what's heard
            With hands at their fire.
And lo, in face of a caller, suddenly shier,
      The youngest hovers before his kiss.

Visitation

        You never met my sons,
    You were long gone before they were born,
            But just before the dawn
     Today, just as I sensed the sun's
Proximity, you called to me as I passed
To make sure they'd come say goodbye at last.

        You looked younger than when
    I saw you last, in your translucence
            At the end, your fingers loosened
    On mine. I saw you talked with friends.
The place I recognized as a border town;
A sign said, it was once a pleasure ground.

        I hesitate to write
    About a dream, but now I see
            I passed through Purgatory
    The very end of last night
And the only way to get back there now
With my sons is along these lines somehow.

        So, here's the eldest one,
    Called Ludovico: he collects
            Fossils and rocks; he's vexed
    By his socks; his hair is straight and blond;
He hasn't found, he says, his talent yet,
Although he would be horse-riding, I'll bet.

        And here is Iacopo,
    Who lives up to his ancient name
            Royally, and looks the same
    As me: the curly one who'd know
On entering your home with a mind that glints
The whereabouts of your stash of sweets and mints.

Ten years ago, I tried
　　To fashion you an elegy
　　　　　From a rill of Purgatory,
　　But it never quite satisfied.
My father craved a villanelle for his mum.
What must he make of this adventurous poem?

The Infinite Sum

        The god who gets me up so early
                To figure out this poem
        Might be the god of my response
                To a dire homework sum
When I was so distraught but looked as surly
As an old king who loved his daughters once.

        God of the gods of the fraught start
                To all of my school years
        The end of those majestic Augusts,
                And guardian of the tears
That welled when my mum's disbelief would dart
Like fire of angels and I tried to focus:

        How close was your manifestation
                At our long wooden table
        Before the cockerels in the painting
                When I was quite unable
To see the concept of multiplication
My little sister grasped while she sat waiting.

        Now that my own son burns and pines
                To answer each hard sum
        And blanks and stares while I begin
                To rage just like my mum,
So teach us to number the sum of these lines
That we can hear his knock and let him in.

The Great Threshold

    The board was a round man: I leaned toward him
    And channelled through the upheld feinting dart
    The spirit of Andy "The Viking" Fordham
    And prodded at the mystery of his heart
    With fingers used to tools of another art.
    I concentrated hard, collected my faults,
    Through intervening air, made out a chart.
    A clear and certain aim gets the results.
A dart sweeps with a flight no fake or false fowl moults.

    Once the first husky was secured, the pressure
    Was on to win another for the son
    Who looked on, daring to believe he'd treasure
    The same plush dog, I had already won
    For his big brother, and so, one by one,
    Six more bits of the day were taken up,
    And weighed for what they were, and thrown upon
    That board, the border of the fair's hubbub,
And the next day each son took round his ghost-white pup.

No Picnic

What is the context for this work? I've led
                You to believe these things
Are taken from life, but now it must be said
I live my life as at the end of Kings,
                And I shall make this poem
From broken treasures of Jerusalem.

I lie down by the Thames and watch clouds mass
                Expressing visions of God,
When all at once my children cycle past
Then leave their bikes to paddle in the mud.
                The waters murmur round,
I eat my roll, and listen to their sound.

Arise, deliver me from men of the world
                Enclosed in their own fat
Whose bellies are full of your treasure and children curled
In shapes of hedgehog and dragon round that:
                I pray you send again
An angel to seal their mouths as you sealed this den.

After the picnic my thoughts take leave and go
                Like shepherds through the hills
Or poets of a hundred years ago
Who went to live in their tower, and my cup fills
                With blackberries I pick,
And I see how the world's grown restlessly sick.

Gloria in excelsis, I heard told
                The angels say, or sing,
And my stripped sons cry out to wade in the cold
And they behold the face of a newborn king.
                What fickle messengers
Are these whose backs seem turned to clouds at my prayers?

No Mercy Seat

And when he cried again with a loud voice
      Recalling, this time, no psalm or hymn
           And the veil was rent with the noise
           Where were the cherubim
      And Ark, but in a cave, they say,
You could not find, although they'd marked the way.

It was Jeremiah who took them there, it's said,
      When the first Temple was destroyed,
           And with wings stretched over head
           They might match my shed's toys
      Aslant on heaps where they've been shoved
By tins of paint and bikes, exiled and unloved.

And when the second Temple was razed too,
      Not long after his final cry,
           Was it so we'd see through
           His broken heart on high?
      So some kind of atonement can
Be found in these words squared in shape of a man?

Before these fabled temples there was just
      A tent where Moses could commune
           With God from out the dust
           Of desert ground. In tune
      At last each cherub looks on the other
And plays, or wrestles, brother on laughing brother.

Sphinges

I

        It was at first, and still today might be,
                A page that chance
                Has opened on,
    Or synchronicities to make me glance
            From some or other activity.
                But was it ever poured
        As wisdom once into Solomon?
Often it felt a pair of angels soared
                Down through the dead of night
            To take the childish forms on my page,
                With me poised to break their fight,
Afraid of such obvious ecstasy and rage,
        And often like mystic psalms and hymns
My own sons came down and fused with these cherubims.

If I could see their face the very stones
                Would spin down from
            Their edifice
Of plaster, egg, and pigment, onto my poem.
        In their apocalyptic bones
                Each part of scripture greets
            Another with open artifice.
They call and all allusion sits and eats—
                Immediately, with hands
        Already washed, making no fuss.
            I see the promised lands
Of refused words of love's *midrash* and trust
        My children shall rest and hold sway in that place
Where head stones and fir trees are crying out their praise.

II

    We call these sphinges cherubims
    But that transliteration hardly does
    Them justice if you see some chubby limbs
    Or disembodied toddlers' heads above us:
    No, they're fierce fighters, these winged creatures, primed
    For the touch of your feet on the grotesque shrine.

    You see them stood up on pendentives, poised
    To draw all thoughts of what they represent
    Right back to heaven like words purged of our noise:
    The quartered end of a tetramorph that's sent
    To shelter the source text of all source texts,
    These creatures are sensed like an awareness you're next.

I look up *tetramorph,* since it's proclaimed on the back
This new dictionary's the foremost authority on English,
But find between *tetrameter* and *Tetra Pak*
No *union of attributes of four evangelists*
In one winged creature, as it's put in my old *Concise,*
And wonder if the word's fallen into disuse.

    Or if there is a plan to quite erase
    Our knowledge of Christian art so that
    We see but perceive not what desolates
    The land and makes the heart of people fat:
    Those sphinges at the corner of the eye
    Whose faces are the words of your life on high.

    What are these cherubim that play by the door
    In expectation of a visitor's knock,
    But a veil I see rent from roof to floor
    And living substance of our holiest book:
    They are the very couch on which I write,
    Which climbs on all fours round my house by night.

Keep listening but do not comprehend.
Keep looking but please, please don't understand.
Bring it on, faster and faster near the end,
And don't you dare look up from the phone in your hand,
For vast is the emptiness in the midst
Of the land and heavy the sight if you lift your lids.

Initiation

        Sporadically children appear,
   And if the priest's reciting, each one makes
      Gestures for the next to come near,
            But for Christ's sake
            Without a sound,
And when the baby grand's pulled out, they all stand round
    On sawn up pallets the choir mistress found.

       Kyrie eleison—
Don't shout—*Christe*—stop there—*ele*—I, I—
    Ison—OK. I want each one
          Of you to try
          Again, and sing
This time—and so it goes on, the choir practising
    The *Kyrie* and then some other things.

      O Lord, have mercy, Christ, be gracious,
   And hear them when they cry and practise their call:
    This song that makes the soul so spacious
          It fills with all
        Of those who've cried
Its words before, from David to beggars by the wayside
   Who were blind and made whole before you died.

      Since this tradition is maintained
  Of singing the *Kyrie* at Mass, a truth's
    Dispersed, no discourse could profane,
         And children, youths
         And adults feel,
As they sing, the touch of living creatures on their wheel,
   And this poem's made for those who see they're real.

Navicularius

He held the boat in hands so capable,
                       While his brother's mate's
Brother tossed and threw round the thurible;
                       His upturned face
Shone as it were the face of an angel: our son's,
Who later gave a thumbs up and yawned through no songs.

His elder brother and his lively mate
                       Were *ceroferari,*
And you and the other mother sat and faced
                       Them all, as wary
As guards of Eden the far side of the choir,
And gazed on them with loving eyes of fire.

The speakers in the church were so distorted
                       With fulgent feedback,
You'd have to look the readings up, they snorted
                       Right to the back
Of the echoing nave, to have a text to hold
And cradle like him in the dark of this poem's hold:

Our curly little *navicularius*
Who served for the first time last week, without fuss.

Zoomorphism

Why don't you write them down
And with a flick of the wrist
Let's see what can't be done.
Even if it's a long list,
Who knows they'll not have vanished
In a puff of deadlines
As you stare at things to be finished:
That piece of work, these lines,
Your very life, I'd say,
As you lie down the end
Of another long day;
All those worries that rend
The garments of your heart
And have begun to tear
The hours up of your art,
And vex you everywhere.

The smoke recedes and there
He stands resplendently
On the very top stair
In his zoomorphic tee
And brand-new monkey slippers:
That vast cherubic poem,
Who'd torn through ripped up papers
On the floor of our trashed home
And asks now, what's for breakfast.
Though I rise in the midst of trouble,
The sight of that living nexus
Makes me reel and see double,
And clasp the hand of the Psalmist,
Who'd lain afar off in bed
In spiderman pyjamas,
Spell-bound in words I'd read.

Contentation

You heard it said that we can do all things
                Through Christ, and laughed to think
That you would eat nothing but chocolate cake
                All this week in that case,
                      And that therefore
You'd not be going to school anymore.

But truly, you'd do well to mind this text
                Next time that you're sat vexed
At a high price put in your maths homework
                And press toward its mark,
                And let me add,
In what state you are, be content with that.

Learn to love your littleness, to be poor
                In spirit, and on the door
To your soul you'll hear the knock of a teacher come
                In the fire of your hard sum
                    To help you see,
You are at once the problem and its key.

The Night

John 3:8

You spoke by night and formed your thoughts
    To the pattern of an old ballad or psalm,
Like one to which a mother has recourse
    When she'd her colicky baby calm:
With opened eyes, he sees her and sits up;
To a tune she'd heard a month ago, his back's rubbed.

My son looks up with glistening eyes
    Each night I do the voice as he asked it
Of Ratface Rodney, or ventriloquize
    The bear and goat in *The Shopping Basket,*
Or Smudge in *Mrs Armitage:* each week
He picks a new book to hear the fresh rogues speak.

Except a reader's born from above
    He cannot give his voice to the text
And those that speak it: those ghosts that move as a dove
    When you don't know what you'll say next:
Except a reader's born again, and again,
How can he take the tablet, or pad and pen.

The Hunt for the Soul

      Who knows the power of his anger?
          When I have drowned a son
      In waves of mine and sensed his rancour
          Is a spirit that looks on,
That question cries for a tale to be told
          Like those we heard of old.

      But all I have is a mean style
          That would present a slice
      Of life, and an infant hope I'll
          Write that and then be nice.
I clasp my hands together to the light
          And my voice shakes with fright.

      One day, I hope, my sons shall make
          The anger of their fears
      Into a spiritual form to take
          Through their declining years,
And they shall find each passionate event
          Is a creature heaven sent.

      But O how hard to mould the lump
          Of that time I yelled in your face,
      And breathe upon the tears I thumbed
          And the red cheek I traced,
To make a living soul to whom I say
          Come with me today.

The Net

These words don't pace about and testily stress
About the state of our house; they're not annoyed
When they tread on the train or skirts of its mess,
The carpets cluttered like the plains of Troy
With heaps of clothes, abandoned gear, and toys;
And they're not vexed when there's a meal to cook
And dirty dishes everywhere they look.

These lines don't spoil for a fight when they're tired
And argue for the sake of argument;
They do not spend the small hours sitting wired
And strung out on their couch to catch what's sent
From out the empyrean's flowing element;
But they are lying by your side to touch
Your lips and feel the heat of your cherishing clutch.

These verses pray you turn to them and take
Their rhymes and uncouth iambs into the arms
Of your tongue, to murmur them out and make
Them sweet as Samson's honey, strong as charms
Medea spoke, and those drummed on dry farms.
This poem is cast on what looks so serene
And writhes with things hardly dreamt of or seen.

Steel

I look in dictionaries because I care
Primarily about the age of the word
And then I turn to a poem about a sword;
I look around, move room, and everywhere
I look this hard material is there:
In the cook's knife and the knife on the breadboard,
In pans and appliances, we use and hoard;
I look and think of washing up as I stare.
Words clash with thoughts and sound like steel on steel
And knives and pans I've put on the plate rack
Bring all our kitchen conversations back
To the glistening role of this metal in each meal.
I hold the hand of each monster argument
We've had aloft and wonder what was meant.

The Marriage

For Andy and Nassim

As I unzipped the garment bag
To change before the wedding
I saw that pierced lapels had been festooned
With white cocoons,
And there could be no doubt,
As I shrunk back to let a moth fly out,
My suit was now a holy rag
Whose wings were swiftly spreading.

I was speechless, but quickly sought
My only other suit,
While my wife flapped round frantically to try
And hurriedly dry
Her glistening dark red nails.
Our children played, then stopped to fight, then wailed,
And all is vanity, I thought,
As I dusted off a boot.

Our taxi crunched the gravel drive
Causing some guests to miss
The Rumi I later learned was being read
Over our heads,
But we made it in time
To see them married: these old friends of mine
Amongst the trees, blessed to survive
The blaze of Maytime's bliss.

Of the End of the World

I was looking for the story that described
        The marriage feast of the King's son,
In sympathy with the man who had arrived
        Without a wedding garment on,
But the book opened chapters later at
The end of the world, and I thought, well, I'll read that.

Strange to say, only the day before, we'd all
        Gone to see a crumbling church,
Which had that scene painted on its north wall,
        And I saw there, while my dad perched
And my youngest lolled upon a pew and talked
Of God, all nations marked like faintest strokes of chalk.

The panorama, literally as wide
        As hell and high as heaven, put forth
Its leaves, although it was winter outside
        And a keen rain blew from the north:
I could just make out a striped angel that stirred
A crowded pot and figures flocked like starving birds.

At the end of the world there's still time to impart
        A tale or so to remind us to
Keep ourselves provided with visionary art
        And words that can accommodate you
As when two figures knocked at a thatched place
And were so received the wine welled up like a shining face.

Plate 21

To make the happy ending, so I'm told,
      We're shown again in the last plate
The same family group as in the first.
But I arrived at the print shop too late
      And the last plate had been sold,
The fine series in process of being dispersed.

I turn to the first and see Blake's Job with a book
      On his lap, his back against the rough
And twisted bark of the fat tree of life
As the wind plays quaintly thin strings above,
      And dream of how I'd curl in a nook
Or corner or dell before I'd sons and a wife.

These days I write on my couch and hear the noise
      Of living creatures above as they
Awake and call to me and sneeze and stretch.
But I know that after breakfast they'll play
      The doxology I crave: my boys
Who make me rise as if I'd my harp fetch.

Banqueting House

We'd put the sherry out with a mince pie
When suddenly beside the hearth my boys
Began to dance on a vast spontaneous high

In expectation of tomorrow's toys
(I snapped a shot of them to share online).
The mouse disdained the cheddar we'd tried to foist

On her but left a coin for the canine
When we put a piece of parmesan with it
Next evening (her taste is so refined).

We lay these banquets out and hope they'll visit,
Take the tooth, and bless our house with gifts,
These fays in whose presence I am complicit.

But who would dare to sup with him who sifts
Like winnowing wind these words I've scythed and let cry,
That stranger on this threshold whose shape shifts?

About the Author

Edward Clarke was born on the edge of the Forest of Dean in 1975. After attending schools in Lydney, Buenos Aires, and Monmouth, he studied English Language and Literature at St Catherine's College, Oxford, and then undertook a PhD on Wallace Stevens at Trinity College, Dublin. He now lives in Oxford with his Italian wife and two sons, teaching English literature and art history at various colleges and the Department for Continuing Education at Oxford University. His collection of poems, *A Book of Psalms,* was published by Paraclete Press in 2020. 'Clarke's Psalter,' the documentary he presented about writing these poems, was broadcast on BBC Radio 4 in September 2018. A selection of his poems, called *The Voice inside Our Home,* was published at the beginning of 2022 by SLG Press. He is also the author of two books of criticism, *The Later Affluence of W. B. Yeats and Wallace Stevens* (Palgrave Macmillan, 2012) and *The Vagabond Spirit of Poetry* (Iff Books, 2014).

www.ingramcontent.com/pod-product-compliance
Lightning Source LLC
Chambersburg PA
CBHW022145160426
43197CB00009B/1432